The Program

The Program

MEGAN FENNYA JONES

icehouse poetry
an imprint of Goose Lane Editions

Edited by Dorothea Lasky.
Cover and page design by Julie Scriver.
Cover image by Matt Moloney, unsplash.com.
Printed in Canada by Coach House Printing.
10 9 8 7 6 5 4 3 2 1

Library and Archives Canada Cataloguing in Publication

Title: The program / Megan Fennya Jones.
Names: Jones, Megan Fennya, author.
Description: Poems.
Identifiers: Canadiana 20220209057 | ISBN 9781773102528 (softcover)
Classification: LCC PS8619.O53345 P76 2022 | DDC C811/.6—dc23

Goose Lane Editions acknowledges the generous support of
the Government of Canada, the Canada Council for the Arts,
and the Government of New Brunswick.

Goose Lane Editions is located on the unceded territory of the Wəlastəkwiyik
whose ancestors along with the Mi'kmaq and Peskotomuhkati Nations signed
Peace and Friendship Treaties with the British Crown in the 1700s.

Goose Lane Editions
500 Beaverbrook Court, Suite 330
Fredericton, New Brunswick
CANADA E3B 5X4
gooselane.com

For Nigel

Contents

INSIDE OUT

With minimal effort
I can leave my body
to watch it move
through the world
Many women
have discussed this phenomenon
so I will not go into detail
or pretend I am special
but I will say
my ability is advanced
I spend more time out here
than I do in there
Soon I will not need to return at all
I will stay out here
I will make a home out here

A SEASON IN HELL

I carry a heavy book of photos
All the photos are of me
I wait for the métro
I put on stilettos
I watch men
consider the photos
raise their white têtes
and consider me
I perform myself
I say, I write poetry
From the warmth of his lap I say
Ô sorcières, ô misère, ô haine!
I say
A less blazing eye!
as he shoots me on his bed
in head-to-toe Lanvin I'm dying
At the café I do not mange
At the café I throw the bread
to the pigeons!
At the café I'm reading Zadie Smith's *On Beauty*
At the café I'm reading Ezra
Pound
At the café I'm writing
I walk out of the métro
and another model hangs herself
I walk out of the métro
and two more leap from a building
I walk out of the métro
and I have voir so much already
I have voir the top of my tête
emerging from
different holes
sur la ground
I march up the métro steps

into the starry nuit
into the camera's blazing
eye
I march up the men's laps
to tickle their white têtes
I march up the men's laps
all the way to Père Lachaise
all the way to Morrison's disappointing
grave
I march down the men's laps
into the black gleam
into the Paris of my dreams

INTAKE EXAM

Do you have frequent disturbing thoughts?
Define disturbing
Like grotesque images for example
This psychiatrist seems like someone
who should be more attracted to me
I wore my little bra, my best shoes
the ones with the clean soles
that click on his hospital floor
He walks me past a white tube
with a girl attached to it
Her eyes fly open
like two screen doors
I feel myself withering
I feel myself becoming
a grotesque image for example
I eat a brown thing
from the psychiatrist's tray
and say I'm ready for the Program
Do you have the will to survive?
Define survive
Your body existing in the future

BLACK LAKE

There's a sound in my sheets
my busted laptop
a dead knocking
I move it to the floor
It's true that I am inwardly
screaming
I make my heart into a black lake
and row through the lily pads
wailing
Björk said women are like atoms
the small bits that stick
all the big things together
But the world dismantled me so handily
like all those good mechanics
saying *This old girl*
She won't run again
Take the good parts for yourself
Build a shed somewhere
Let someone else nail her
back together

THE PROGRAM

Sad girls in sweatpants
move through the halls
like gusts of sour-smelling wind
My caseworker has the same name
as my childhood best friend
Kyla
She explains that the thing I do
at night when I am alone
is not what we're here to *work on*
That thing is *the tip of the iceberg*
In the Program we will discover
what's underneath
I imagine Kyla and I
feeling up an iceberg
in the gloom
Green shimmering slime
oozes from a gaping hole
and I put my finger in it
Hey
this work will be painful
At times it will make you hate me
Are you ready?

FISH POEM

I took a cab to your studio tonight
because I decided not to go home with Tobias
He showed me photos of the inside
of Taylor Swift's apartment
and said she was too famous to love
Tobias writes love songs for pop stars
He wrote one for me once
and it pulled me to him like a fish
hooked by its eye
After dinner he pinned me against a wall
with his hand on my throat
It all felt like the dark pull
of a familiar tide
I'm telling you this now because I have a fantasy
where I hurl my body at the tide
so you can drag it out, wet and glistening
But you're not that kind of person
and you have a painting to finish
so I walk home from your studio alone
leave the door unlocked for you
I write this poem before I fall asleep
because its voice is another body in the house

UNDERSTANDING PAINTINGS

You say I don't understand paintings
because I'm expecting too much

You tell me to describe
only what I'm actually seeing

I see a red line
A screen door

I see a white machine
A dark hallway

Being deaf and nearly seven feet tall
you say to be yourself

is to be an artist

You say nothing new is out of bounds
when you're already out of bounds

You dress in monochrome
Big black boots

Silver hearing aids
curl around your ears

You look really good
A waiter says it best: *Welcome to the Matrix*

We see each other on Thursdays
Decide what you like, you say

and demand only this
Make a list of every perfect thing in the world

and covet every single one

The first time you asked me to kiss you
I declined

You don't kiss your teacher ;)

THE PROGRAM

Kyla signs me up for classes
with astonishing names
Food and Feelings
Tame Your Inner Gremlin
I don't feel worthy
of my own attention
It's too much
and the bodies of the sad girls
are too real
the soft pillows of their stomachs
expanding with every breath
The air in the room
hammers against my skin
I miss the girl with the white tube
her tight, white sheets
her translucent teeth
I close my eyes
and her bare face
hangs above me like a moon
Kyla grabs my hand then
and pulls me deeper
where it is even colder

JOE BLOW

He drives like Paris is a film
he saw once and didn't like
Fingers tapping the wheel
Eyes on his phone
He takes me dancing
when I am fourteen
when I am seventeen
when I am twenty-one
He parks in the back
He takes me home
to watch *The Sixth Sense*
He is a Buddhist
He is a Christian
He is a Muslim
He is sober
around so many drunk girls he says
I like to keep them safe
He is from Italy
He is from Morocco
He is from Spain
We call him Uncle
We call him Daddy
He is big and bald
with firm brown skin
We call him Buddha
We call him Baby
He owns the club
so we have to be good
or he won't let us in
He is the only person
we know with a car
I am in his car feeling like
a manta ray
gliding low

and slow
over Pont Neuf
I am in his car
lit up like his console
I love changing his CD
feet on the dash
He says *put them down*
He is my French Daddy
I want to go
home he says *you're a*
good girl he
takes me to get candy
in his glowing buttery car

HIGHWAYS IN SPAIN

I ask you about an artist
in a book I'm reading
who lays his paintings like tiles
over highways in Spain
about his girlfriend named Reno
who carves a line in the Bonneville Salt Flats
with her Italian motorcycle
She makes me think of Werner Herzog
trudging from Munich to Paris
to save his friend Lotte
You explain it's called Land Art
The flecks of white paint on the floor
at your studio feel like looking down
at the stars — I want you
to explain things to me
I like it
and you only do it when I ask you to
Yesterday you explained you are sleeping with other people
It was all very relaxed
like how you hold your paintbrush and cigarette
in the same hand
It's also very risky
like imprinting oneself
onto the Bonneville Salt Flats
with an Italian motorcycle
If I were a Land Artist
I would walk to your studio
with my headphones on
I would text *I'm here*
and pull up my jeans
because they are always falling down
I would see myself as you would

from the other side of the glass door
and I would wait for you
to open it

THE PROGRAM

Kyla teaches me to say *symptoms*
I can't say *vomit* or *starvation*
That would be triggering
I can say *Last night I had symptoms*
I can say *I'm hiding symptoms from my boyfriend*
I can say *I'm afraid my symptoms are going to kill me*

VISIT FROM MOTHER

You sleep on the floor in my room
in the modelling apartment
I share with eight other girls
You open the fridge
to see what we're eating
Butter Spray, Diet Coke, Jell-O
Do you think we're clichés
living out of stained suitcases
shaving our legs with shampoo
carving our names into bed-frames
We clog the sink with hair
Our hair is everywhere!
Heather locks herself in the bathroom
Priscilla sleeps on the couch
Barbara goes out
and never comes back
I'm so ashamed of you
with your hairy armpits
You make so much noise with your body
breathing and sweating and saying things like
Your safety is my top priority
Marc Jacobs tells you to wait downstairs
while I walk around for them
Next
When I cry you feed me pine nuts
You know what's just enough
and what's too much
A photographer tells you to wait in a café somewhere
He shuts the door and turns the lock
In the photo a shadow
eats half my face
the other half is one big eye
and mouth turned down
like an old petal

THE PROGRAM

I'm allowed out on weekends
so we drop acid
in a yellow field
where a DJ projects neon lights
onto a grove of arbutus trees
You take off your shirt
and I tap your hard stomach
like I'm walking across it
in my fine clean shoes
I ask if my ass has expanded
since I entered the Program
You say my whole body could be better
proportioned
I look up
at the moon and smile
The daisy beside me
is saying something
her blossom heavy and tipped
Chin up she says

DELIGHTFULLY SAD

I will walk to the café instead of driving

A great effort

A woman on roller skates directs traffic

She gives two men the finger for no reason

There are places
I should not be allowed to go

People would be wise
to turn away

Like lightning
it strikes me at intervals

I am electric with it

As a child I loved *Thumbelina*
Thumbelina sleeps in a walnut shell

and waits to fall in love

*I suppose it works best if two people
are about the same size* she says hopelessly

It's a lonely film
for a small child

The world really is too large

Thumbelina barely escapes
an evil beetle who is really a pimp

Lost in a field
she doesn't know her walnut home is nearby

She can't see it
through the giant blades of grass

THE PROGRAM

I wear the same blue dress
day after day
It's wrinkled and misshapen
It's stained with vomit
I sleep in it
Kyla slips me a worksheet
about Personal Hygiene
She holds my hand
and tells me to be brave
In the evening I remove it quickly
intending to keep my eyes closed
but one flies open
like something's caught in it
My body looks dense
like it is a part of history
Is it possible that I am here?
A feeling crashes into me
and I strangle it

AT THE NEW YORK AGENCY

I wear brown leather pants
to have my Polaroids taken
by an intern who says
my legs look like tree trunks
I walk home along Canal
Nobody likes Canal
but I like the ladies selling
knock-off handbags and metal rings
that stain my fingers
In Washington Square Park a homeless man
calls me *beautiful*
and I should be thankful
I should be on the elliptical
splitting my tree trunks
into kindling
In Paris people insulted my body
in a language I didn't understand
That was so nice
That was so necessary
In Paris I could see
I could actually feel
the sky above my head
In Manhattan the buildings are grey hands
pressing the sky away from me

THE PROGRAM

Kyla sits in a chair while I pee
She talks about her daughter
who loooooves to shop
loves leggings and jewel tones
pashmina scarves to wind around her neck
It makes things harder when Kyla watches me pee
It makes me hurt somewhere new
Like my body is a spacesuit I could lift my soul out of
and float away from
but Kyla would hold on to the tiniest wisp of me

I'M IN LOVE WITH YOU

I feel pretty cool eating squid-ink brioche
with sea urchin pâté at the bar

I read somewhere that you can fall back in love
with someone you've fallen out of love with

You just have to love the life you built together
more than the love that leaves

I fell out of love with you yesterday
when you forgot to print my poems at your studio

I fell out of love when my pants fit differently

I fell back in love after that lizard died on TV
and you said the lizard wasn't dead, just sleeping

My landlord tells me in the elevator
about his sympathy morning sickness

When his pregnant wife vomits
he vomits too

I wish you loved me that much
I wish you would vomit next to me

I would vomit next to you

YOUR SKIN IS SO HOT

You pick me up from the Program
winking at the sad girls
We cruise around
Your long hair blows
into my mouth
You yell over the wind
that nothing good can come
from pity
I put my hands under your jacket
Your skin is so hot
I feel that you are the first person
who will leave me for someone else
and I will be devastated
Normally it is me
who does the leaving
and the devastation
We reach an empty parking lot
and hike to a waterfall
You remove my helmet
and I kneel in the dirt
I am pretty good at
getting on my knees
I don't even have to think about it
Kyla says when I'm starving
I can't think I can only do
I can only kneel in the dirt
and look up
with a dick in my mouth
Kyla tries to make me think
up new words like *boundaries*
vulnerability and *self-respect*
But it's not until you are inside me
that my thoughts get loose
like coins in a pocket

I can touch them and move them around
I can really see them
I can see *privacy respect safety*
if I want
or I can see
a grotesque image for example

PARIS ASSIGNMENT

The makeup artist hands me a straw
so I can sip water without ruining my lipstick
The photographer invites me
to take off my shirt
The stylist says *you don't have to*
as he takes off my shirt
I kneel on concrete
No lie on your back
I lie on my back
Put your finger in your mouth
The stylist turns away
He is disgusted or
packing up his kit I am
somewhere up high
near the ceiling the shutter
opens and closes and
It looks difficult
down there on the ground
She seems to really need the blaze
of the eye on her face
but she also needs
someone to cradle her head
The concrete under her skull
is so cold
She will never carry
this photo in her heavy book
Her small breasts
will glimmer
in some dark corner
of the internet
then go out

SAFEWAY

I am holding a bag of carrots
in the candy aisle
watching the girl from *Food and Feelings*
dip her fingers
into the bin of chocolate almonds
and emerge with handfuls
that go into her mouth
I want to tell her about the girl from the hospital
whose fingers lie still in her lap
whose psychiatrist stands at her bedside
day after day
like a bored Victorian lover
More than anything I want to tell her
that the produce boys here
will let her use their bathroom
and the fan is so loud
she won't hear herself vomiting

HOUSE-SITTING FOR MY AUNT

We feed her chickens, rake her leaves
kiss in her small yellow kitchen
I'm writing about black lakes
and you are starting a series of paintings
about skydivers
I ask why and you say
I want to go skydiving
When my aunt comes home
I move into her spare room
You stop coming by
and a girl you're sleeping with
confronts me at your art show
She wants me to kiss her in front of you
I do and you don't notice
So I buy your largest painting for one hundred dollars
but forget to shut the chicken coop
One sticks her head under a two-by-four and dies
In the morning we throw her on the compost heap

THE PROGRAM

To empty and empty again
to treat my body like a wide chute
down which rain and dark shapes rattle
This continues to be a radical act for me

REJECTION LETTER

Standing in line at Trader Joe's I receive a rejection letter
from a publisher where my friend is the editor

He describes a lack of figurative language and too much
this happened, then this happened

So we go and visit the Glossier store and see face creams
travel through a pipe in the ceiling

We take an Uber and the driver
tells me I speak too slowly

At the New York City Ballet performance
of *A Midsummer Night's Dream*

we watch women move across the stage
like they're forging a powerful river

A man follows
like a toy boat bobbing in their wake

When it's over I stand and clap even though
I recognize the man from a #MeToo article

In a video you took of me that night
I am running up a set of subway steps
holding the bottom of my blue dress in one hand

At the top I turn left and right, bewildered
by the crush of bodies, the bright lights

When I finally look back, I see you and smile
understanding how ridiculous I look

THE PROGRAM

Kyla says my eating disorder
is a log floating in a river
that I have held on to for many years
to stop myself from drowning
But now the log is dragging me
downstream
to my death

LOVE SONG

You take me to Greece
because travel is good for my health
I love to lose weight
walking on all these cobbled streets
Why is it so hard for me to be good for you?
I have everything I need
to live long and prosper
but I throw my privilege in the face of the world
I tiptoe into the kitchen we share
with the couple from Belgium
to pour extra cream in your coffee
I want to plump you up
like a baklava
I want to close like a clam
on the ocean floor
I want to silence the voice
that screams DANGER
as the waiter floats toward me
swinging his silver tray
like a scythe

THE BEACH TODAY

I love this guy's chest tattoo
FOREVER LOVER

Lying here on hot sand the backs of my knees are sweating

like when I come and you say
Now let me feel those knees!

Did you know "Kiss from a Rose"
is about a man eating a woman
out when she's menstruating?

It sounds so lovely
like a hot bun
filled with period blood

LAYER CAKE

I wake in a cold sweat, covered in blood
I've been ripping through super tampons

Is my uterus my womb or does it become my womb
when sperm gets in there?

I would like a womb with me always
sperm or no sperm

Why wouldn't I deserve a dark harbour?
A dank lair layered with sleeping animals?

On the island of Syros, a woman
gives us directions to a cairn

Walk north out of town she says

Follow the highway until you see a cave
where the old man lives with his dogs

Turn left

SATURDAY NIGHT IN PARIS

It's no longer enough
that the sample size fits
It's no longer enough
that each time some Russian in a blue suit
buys me a $20,000 bottle of champagne
I get to spray it in his face
Time is running out
When did my skin become elderly?
When did my eyes become my hands
my ears, my mouth?
I stand before the mirror
talking to the intern on the phone
She suggests *running a bath*
I try to imagine a body
that would do such a thing
My pubic mound is a black hole
between two bloated legs
Earlier I used a hand
to make myself vomit
I wanted to see inside this body
all the way to its end

VISIT TO THE COUNTRY

Marlot, the girl who rents monthly
from the Elk Valley Motel

heals horses for a living
She can diagnose a sick horse

from miles away
Put the phone up to her muzzle

she says into the receiver
Let me hear her breathe

Marlot's patients have pop-star names
Fancy, Nova, Gemma, Star

I watch her wedge one shoulder
into Gemma's flank, wipe snow

from her mitt and lift the foreleg
The horse will show you

where to touch and where not to touch
I am a city girl with silly questions

A lot of things seem silly out here
like the words I said to you before I left

Should certain words be kept to oneself?
Probably most words should be fully felt

but never said
Gemma drifts noiselessly along the fence

leaving behind wet clouds
of her generous breath

Marlot keeps two black Angus cows
on a friend's ranch

They don't have names — I mean
she did not think to name them

In March she'll slaughter one
and with the money she'll buy two more

It is so simple and so
violent to earn a living

Marlot's dog is my ideal companion
Good dog, Toad! Toad the dog!

Toad slides over snow
with amphibian grace

I want him to sleep on my bed
but Marlot says he's an outside dog

I invite him up anyway
Why do I ruin everything?

Tractor, sky, barn —
each thing has its own name here

Except for the cows
and the elk who travel like secrets

through the bare trunks of trees

When you pick me up from the airport
I kick your puny tires

Everyone in Elk Valley
drives a truck, I explain

On the way home we are shy
from spending one week apart

The city is cruel, we agree
How can a person build a life here?

I tell you about Marlot, about her tools
that ride in her truck bed

About her multiplying cows
her phone calls with horses

In bed I turn your face to mine
We list the names

of the people we like the most
which is our favourite game

I want to be strong for you
I want to help my cow give birth

pull the wet calf from her belly
and say *It was only a day's work*

I want to know where you hurt
and where you are open

Bodies are real in Elk Valley
Bodies are hard and bright against the snow

THE PROGRAM

I ask Kyla what I have to do
to leave this place
I took off the blue dress
and remained in my body
I ate the potato chips and dip
I saw my thighs touch
in the green light of the iceberg
and stifled a scream
What more does she want?
Kyla says to graduate the Program
I have to return to the sexy psychiatrist
and prove I can eat all the brown things
I have to zip up the spacesuit
and return to Earth
I have to lift one hand off the log
and put it in the water
I have to see the shore

PARIS FASHION WEEK

It was the smell that woke us
that night when the girl
who used to sleep in that bunk
took a shit on the kitchen floor
and wiped it on the walls

The agency sent a man
to carry her body
down the stairs

then he gave us a sponge
a bucket and some bleach
and said something in a language
we didn't understand
but we felt like he was saying
You are children
Just little children

FISH POEM 2

You stop replying to my texts
Despair overwhelms me
like the first time I touched
the iceberg's white underbelly
felt the crushing weight of it
I bike to the beach
bathing suit under my blue dress
I swim fast and strong
as if Kyla were with me
as if I were in her slipstream
A woman on the shore
waves a white towel
at a child in the waves
I look down at my thighs
swaying like two pale fish
and slap them together
to prove they are mine

WHO DECIDES WHO IS BEAUTIFUL?

The girl from the hospital
comes to me in a dream
dragging her white tube behind her
like a broken limb
Who decides who is beautiful? she asks
God?
Wrong
I thought I saw
a blaze of the divine
in the psychiatrist's eye —
oh, why didn't I stay
burning under his microscope?
Instead I came here
to feel the absence of God, of destiny
Who decides who is beautiful?
Mothers? The creators of all beauty?
Wrong
As a child I hid the lunches my mother made
inside my closet
A year later
she found them, rotting
Who decides who is beautiful?
The artists?
Wrong
I let the tongues of artists
slide inside my mouth
The same mouth
that bits of blood and bile come out of
Who decides who is beautiful?
The poets?
Wrong
Do you like my white Givenchy bodysuit
and my grey wig?
I am a whorish Marie Antoinette

I eat M&M's
that make a multicoloured vomit
Who decides who is beautiful?
The philosophers?
Wrong
As Kyla and I tumble down the iceberg
I try to explain how it feels
the blaze of the eye on my face
How it makes me sting
as if I am being pulled from a cold lake
The sting is all I have
and if she takes it from me
I will lose my will to survive
Who decides who is beautiful?
Is it you?
My dream-girl
The one who the psychiatrist stops in front of
on his way to do other things
like a familiar and beloved painting
Wrong
Is it I?
That is, the will to survive?
Yes
To survive is beautiful and real
How does that make you feel?

WALK IN JANUARY

My cup overfloweth

I play "Both Sides, Now"
a hundred times in a row

because Joni makes me cry

I love to cry now
I will cry right in your face

I pass a tree with bark
so thick and so dark

my breath gets stuck going out

Then it springs forth
as from a spring

IT WAS YOUR BIRTHDAY YESTERDAY

Did I tell you I rent a studio now?
I want you to know I am very serious about writing
This morning I told my new boyfriend
I don't know what I'm doing with my life
All I do is cycle to my studio, drink little cups of coffee
and ask my studio mate about her film in which a boy
tries to save a girl from an addiction that seems to be
    improving her life
I go around exclaiming things like
I don't want to make money anymore!
Do you still make paintings?
I really loved your painting of the iPhone 4
on the forest floor
its blank face
upturned and reflecting
black trunks of trees
                  a purple sky
When I am cycling I think
I might die instantly
and I feel a sick little joy

LITTLE FOOT

Kyla, Grandpa keeps chewing
her little foot and making it

look sad. Grandpa is
the name you gave

your grey cat. You say the vet
doesn't know what's wrong

with Grandpa and it makes you sad
to see the little foot

all bloodied and moist
Grandpa wears a cone

and stays home while you
attend your daughter's graduation

I ask what it was like
and you say *small and hot*

Kyla, a nice man
has invited me to live with him

and I feel cornered

I want my days
to remain thick and voiceless

I want to wake up and river
my dark insides

into a silver laptop
and leave it dying on the counter

Kyla, is it inhuman to live
with another person?

Maybe it's very human
and there's something wrong with me

Kyla, you live with your daughter
and Grandpa, one happy family

Kyla, here's the thing
I wake and open the blinds

brew coffee and heat milk
in a saucepan on the stove

I pee with my chin in my hand
careful not to shift

the air in the rooms
careful not to make a new

sound or smell. I want everything
to stay exactly as it was yesterday

and the day before that
and the day before that

because on those days
I wrote something decent

On those days I existed
only in words

Kyla, is it inhumane
to let a person see you?

Is it inhumane to allow
that person to see

you gnaw away at
the small soft parts of yourself?

Kyla, when I was a child
I wanted to live in a tower

gaze at the mirror, smoke cigarettes
and read Ernest Hemingway

When I imagined a future
I was always alone

Kyla, do you ever ask yourself
what happened?

Why does Grandpa ravage her little foot
in the corner of the room?

Is it selfish to invite
a small animal to live with you?

Maybe it's selfless
Maybe Grandpa would have died

if you and your daughter didn't give her
a name. Kyla

I would like to sleep with this nice man
But sex is a small sacrifice

to make for the freedom
to rearrange my dark insides

in a thick and voiceless room
On the other hand, a writer like Hemingway

had plenty of sex and still scattered
so many small abuses

throughout his novels, like coins
turned loose from a pocket

Kyla, when I was young
I studied the works of men

as one studies the plays
of the opposing team

Now I am told
one must read books by women

One must forfeit the game

Kyla, when Grandpa chews
her little foot

does she look lost or
in service of a higher power?

I suppose it's hard to tell
a cat's purpose by how much

she does or doesn't
chew her little foot

Kyla, last night I read
a short story in the *New Yorker*

about a woman who lives
the same day over and over, for eternity

I felt disturbed as I dried my body
and got into bed

as you danced
and drank blood-red wine

at your daughter's graduation,
as Grandpa's little foot

lay bloodied and moist

IT'S HAPPENING AGAIN

So I tape photographs of birds
to the toilet seat
I write *the will to survive*
on the bathroom door
I haven't booked a job in months but my agent says
Nothing has changed
The makeup artist pins my hair over my forehead
because my forehead is freakishly large
I love her soft sounds of disapproval
Insults have always been beautiful
when spoken in another language
I love the stylist's soft hands
as she rolls sheer stockings
up my thighs
I love the camera's manic flash
wake! up! wake! up!
I love the familiar feeling
of floating
How nice it is
to say and do nothing for hours
like you are a part of the wall
or the floor
My mother phones and asks what I ate today
My new therapist calls and asks what I ate today
The food rots in the fridge
The makeup artist rubs my jawbone
to stimulate lymph drainage
I agree with the photographer
when she explains my calves are fat
We cry over breakups, sick pets
We share tips for cosmetic surgery
We say *I love you*
Time gets sticky around the edges

Every day I shed a new layer
and I had been working so hard
to encase my soul in flesh
Is this what Stockholm syndrome feels like?
Maybe
Or maybe this is what happens
when women who are very sick
try to take care of each other

THE PROGRAM

We sit in a circle
We're not allowed to pass the tissues
because Kyla says handing a girl a tissue
is handing her a solution
and there is no solution
There is only *speaking your truth*
I pick my lip until it bleeds
and when I speak my truth I feel blood
flick from my mouth
like the tongue of a snake
then Kyla says
everyone repeat after me:
I know your pain
even as I recognize it as separate and distinct from my own
I send you strength and I have the confidence
that you have the power
and the will to survive

Acknowledgements

Thank you to the wonderful people at icehouse and Goose Lane for editing, marketing, publishing, and distributing this book. Thank you to my editor, Dorothea Lasky, for your generous spirit. Thank you to my mentors, Kayla Czaga and Daniel Zomparelli, for believing in this book. Thank you to Mallory Tater and Curtis LeBlanc for giving me writing community. Thank you to Brandi Bird for your insights. Thank you to Kristen Steenbeeke for being my first reader and my best friend. Thank you to Nigel, I love you. Thank you to my parents. And thank you to Doc, my very good dog.

I gratefully acknowledge the xʷməθkʷəy̓əm (Musqueam), S<u>k</u>w<u>x</u>wú7mesh (Squamish), and səlilwətaɬ (Tsleil-Waututh) peoples on whose land this book was written.

Some of these poems were published previously in the following outlets. Thank you to the editors of each:
"Visit to the Country," *Poetry Northwest*
"Little Foot," *Minola Review*
"Walk in January," Metatron #MicroMeta Series

Megan Fennya Jones is the author of the chapbook *Normal Women*. Her poetry has appeared in journals across North America, including *Poetry Northwest*, *Room*, and *PRISM* international, and was a finalist in the *Minola Review*'s Poetry Contest.

When she was a teenager, Jones worked as a model in Paris and New York, and today she works in independent publishing. *The Program* is her first poetry collection.

Photo by Ian Lanterman